God Chose Me

God Chose Me

Written by

Sophia Levasseur

First Printing: 2019

ISBN 978-1-948581-50-9

Lincross Publishing

Acknowledgments

First, I would like to thank God. God has become everything to me. He has made me who I am today, and without him I'd be nothing. He is the beginner and finisher of my faith, I am who I am because of the goodness of God and my identity rests in who He is. God gave me purpose and employed me full time when all I ever asked for was a 40hr week career. God's faithfulness has exceeded my understanding, I am thankful for his presence in my life. I wouldn't be able to fulfill my purpose without my husband who has helped me and encouraged me along the way. My children who have challenged me to be a better person and who always understand when I have to go away and do what God has called me to do. I'd like to also thank my mother who never gave up on me and still continues to support me. My father who supports my calling. Also, I'd like to thank each and every member of my family, my warrior sisters for their continuous prayers, and my friends for pushing me closer to God. Lastly, I want to thank Apostle Maureen Manoly who mentored me and guided me to the path of purpose.

Dedication

This book is dedicated to those who know there is far more to life than the routine! For anyone who feels stuck even with the degree, the job, or the family, etc. To anyone who carries a dream bigger than you, so big you can't even put into words, this book is for you. I also dedicate this book to the love of my life, my husband. Lastly, I'd like to thank God for choosing me!

God Chose Me

Introduction

"Many are called, but few are chosen" Matthew 22:14 KJV

It was crucial for me to complete this book in obedience to the Holy Spirit. In this book, The Holy Spirit aims to help and guide anyone who is currently living a purposeless life. God our creator made us with a purpose and for a purpose. I almost missed the call of God on my life because I was not living on purpose.

Society claims money is happiness, we buy into the lie that money will solve all of our troubles, that money will make us happy. If that were the case, many celebrities would not commit suicide and therapists would be out of business. Even with all the money in the world, celebrities are not happy, instead they may feel that they are living a purposeless life. Finding and living within your purpose will truly make you happy. Remember, God our creator made us with a purpose and for a purpose. He is the only one who knows the plan for our life. Many people don't have a successful, happy, or purposeful life because they don't seek God's guidance. When you seek God, you receive the key to a life of fullness.

Up until December 2017, I was living outside of God's will for my life, I was living a purposeless life. I was juggling life, hoping that God would make it all work at the end. That was the first mistake. Many of us make plans without consulting God first, then beg him to bless it when our plan doesn't seem to work out. Living in the will of God is the opposite, we consult God first and then walk out the plan in obedience. If you get stuck or have any concerns ask God for help. God is more than willing to help you, afterall, He is the one who has laid out the plans for you. When He sees that you depend on him, He will never leave you stranded.

In the midst of life's trials and tribulations, when life would not go as planned I would ask God and myself, "What did I do wrong to deserve such hardship?" I did not understand then, that God had chosen me. God would use the good, the bad, and the ugly for his glory. I used to see myself as an unlucky person because things seemed to be harder for me. Trials and tribulations made me feel sad and frustrated. I fought harder to complete projects. For instance, a task that would take me six months, my friend would be able to complete it in three months. No kidding! Just my luck! Story of my life! My "luck" was so evident that when my husband and I would begin to plan we'd jokingly say, "You know how our life is set up." Little did I know, our hardship was God's way of telling me that I could not make decisions without getting him involved. All these failures were God's way of telling me that life would be hard without Him. If only I had known the hardships were God's hands upon my life, then I would have been further in life. I would have saved so much money, time, and tears. God's hand upon my life meant I had a call in my life. I had been chosen. God had chosen me!

God Has A Plan

For I know the plan I have for you, declares the Lord, "plans to prosper you and not harm you, plans to give you hope and a future. Jeremiah 29:11 NIV

I was born in 1983 in Port-au-Prince, Haiti to a single mom. Growing up in Haiti with one parent to provide was difficult, but my mom made it work. I went to a great school and my mother worked enough to help us scale into the middle class in Haiti. Haiti has a very "social class" oriented culture, but even though we were in middle class it never felt like it. My mom struggled and carried most of the burden. It was hard to watch my mom carry most of the weight, I always wonder what our lives would have been like if my father would have been around. I once held unto pain but now I can say I have forgiven my father for abandoning my mom, while pregnant to marry someone else. Although it was not easy, I was able to forgive my father because God forgave us first and thankfully our circumstances don't surprise God.

God knows everything about us. He formed us in our mother's womb and has a plan in place to prosper us and not harm us. So many times we make plans which don't come to pass because ultimately, God has the last word. He calls the shots, we don't know the specifics to God's plans for us, what we do know is that his plan is for the best. Being led by God for direction is so important. When we are led by God we understand that there are no bad situations, just productive steps into our calling. Even when we make bad choices, God is able and almighty to help us learn and push forward to our full potential in Him. Jeremiah 29:11 reminds us, "For I know the plan I have for you, declares the Lord, "plans to prosper you and not harm you, plans to give you hope and a future." The word of God reminds us that He knows the plan! We have a calling, YOU have a calling! It doesn't matter what social group you belong to, what country, what language, what culture, or how many bad experiences you may have gone through. God knows who YOU are, He has a plan set in place just for YOU.

God had a plan in place for my mother. My mother comes from a two parent home but lost her mother at a young age. Growing up without a mom was not easy for her, although her father was a great provider to all of his kids, my mother always felt like her life would've been so much more different if her mom would've been by her side. Fortunately, all the trials and tribulations made her the woman she is today. Though my mother did not understand, God knew. His plans for her would help her prosper, give her hope, and a future (Jeremiah 29:11).

My mother's name is Jeanne Elsy Dutreuil, she was born in the Southern part of Haiti. She is the fourth of eight siblings. After graduating High School, my mother moved from the countryside of Haiti to the city in Port-au-Prince for better opportunities. Most of my mother's siblings also did the same, they left home to the unknown in pursuit of a better future. But before moving to Port-au-Prince, they went to school to a nearby city where there was better school than the city where they came from. They lived in someone's home and that adult would care for their well being. Her time away from home marked her life forever, much of her personality stems from the mistreatment she endured during that time. My mother hated the place she was in, so during school breaks she would return home. My grandfather worked hard to provide for his children but was very strict. My mother tried many times to explain the mistreatment she was receiving but her Dad would not believe her, so she endured the pain for years.

My mother's story is painful, but God has a great way of orchestrating things for our good, to bring us to our purpose. He knows exactly what experiences my mother had to go through to shape and mold her into who she needed to be and consequently who I needed to be. Who we are is directly attached to our parents background, experiences, personalities, and so on. That is why God said in Jeremiah 1:5, "Before I formed you in the womb I knew you." All the events that took place in your mother, grandmother, and great grandmother's life happened so God could use them for His glory.

The life my mother endured shaped her so much that it still affects her today. Although she is responsible, respectful, honest, and loving she is also afraid. For example, my mother has been faithful in her workplace for over 35 years. Even if she were guaranteed a higher paying job she would not take it because my mother is afraid of the unknown. Here's another example, I have encouraged her to purchase a new car, but she won't do it. She is constantly thinking of "what if" scenarios. What if the car payment is too high? What if the new car breaks down? etc. Though it is wise to be cautious, living in fear is not. On the other hand, I understand why she is so cautious in life. I believe her experience of not having a mom, living away from home, and a strict father has stirred fear in her. Nonetheless, my mother is kind and persistent. Her entire life has consisted of putting others before her. My mother's environment and experiences shaped her identity. In the midst of it all, God was there watching, taking notes, executing orders, sometimes in silence- so his plan could come to pass. Even then, God was already thinking of me, Sophia. Through the ups and downs of Jeanne Elsy Dutreuil, He was going to deliver his great plan.

My mother was in a relationship with my father for three years before she got pregnant. Shortly after she got pregnant, my father left her to marry someone else. As if that weren't hard enough, when I was seven months old, I was hospitalized for several days and nearly died. Yet again, my mom persisted. After experiencing abandonment from my father, my mom never initiated a new relationship nor conceived another child. I don't blame her, Can you imagine the pain of being alone? The fear of not being able to trust again? and all the anger, resentment, and rejection in the process? If the pain is so evidently seen now, can you imagine the pain then, while carrying a child in the womb? It's sad and I personally don't think she has been able to surpass the pain of her circumstances.

As a mother of three, I can testify that there is no greater pain than to be pregnant and abandoned by the father of your child. During pregnancy, a woman goes through physiological, emotional, and physical changes. And as you may already know, Science suggests that a fetus can feel their mother's emotions. I believe that my mother's pain at that time of conception affected me. Yet still, God had a plan for me and He was going to use my mother's tribulations for His glory. I am not sure if I was conceived in pain but I was growing through pain in my mother's belly. God was creating a new thing, He was strengthening me through my weakness. The call on my life required extra strength and from conception God was setting me apart. Jeremiah 1:5 reminds us, "Before I formed you in the womb I knew you, before you were born I set you apart; I appointed you as a prophet to the nations." Life are not mere circumstances, if you take the time to review and analyze the trajectory of your life, you will begin to see a pattern or a common thread. Despite the pain and confusion in your life, God

STILL has a plan for YOU, he has set you apart.

Pain is not something we tend to want to deal with, most of the time we ignore it or feed into it. Our lack of trust in God makes us impatient, we want to pray the pain away or wish it away. When in all reality, God is working it out for our good. Pain is equal to purpose. God uses your pain to lead you into your purpose, He allows his grace to cover you and mold you. Don't run away from God's plan for your life. There is a reason behind your suffering, don't run away from the pain, remember His plans will prosper you. My mother is a prime example of staying the course. Although she did not understand God's plan through the pain, she literally carried his plan and chose his grace before her selfish desires. She could have easily taken the easy way out and aborted the process, but she trusted God. My mother chose grace. The same way God chose me, my mother chose me too.

Many times, we feel like God cannot use us due to our dirty and messy past, but God has already chosen YOU. God loves to use people who don't have it all together because He can then shine through you. His power can shine through you. God is the creator of all things and as so, wants to get all the glory even through your mess. Human beings tend to take the blame and the credit for the things that happen in their life but God says "NO, My grace is sufficient for you" It is God who gives you the strength and the one who aligns all things for your good. That is why it is important to align yourself with God so you can know his will for your life.

Remember, when you are chosen by God, the devil will do anything and everything in his power to destroy you. The sooner the better. The devil's job is to distract you and steer you away from God's plan. Don't let bad situations keep you away from God's will. God is our creator, He is almighty, and He knows how to correct every situation that the devil has created to use against us. Trust God, believe that He is the creator. He is the Alpha and Omega. What can take you one year to do, God can do it in one day! Remember, trust God in your situation. Follow his will for your life, stay the course, and know that He has chosen you. There is no better life than the one that aligns with his will.

My Childhood

Growing up, my mother did the best she could. I was my mother's only child and she did everything and anything to provide for my needs. My mother managed to put me in one of the best schools in the country and was able to put a roof over my head. Her resources and income were limited, but my mom always found a way. It's hard now not to have seen God's hand over my mom, but it was. The roof over our head was home to many, many of my cousins and uncles lived with us. In our home, I was the youngest and most of the attention was placed on me. Many could say I was spoiled, but I was far from it. I was blessed with lots of affection, God blessed me with what I needed during my childhood. Now I ask myself all the time how my mom was able to provide with such scarce resources and income. I thank God for providing strength and opportunities for my mom. My mom became the best version of herself through God's love and direction.

I grew up having everything I needed but not everything I wanted. Yet people still assumed I was spoiled. Being an only child automatically gave me the title of "Spoiled" when in fact, that was very far from the truth. As an only child I received so much attention and affection, so much so that I grew up with many insecurities. If I could, I would have preferred a sibling. I wish I could have shared my mother's love, my toys, and my room, rather than growing up in loneliness. I would have loved an annoying sister to play with rather than neighbors to play a game or two. Even now, I wish I had a brother or sister to confide in. Building friendships today is still very new and uncomfortable. I have spent many years alone as an only child, but God knew best. God had a purpose in my life. He designed it perfectly for where He was taking me. The insecurities formed from when I was a child helped me lean into music. I began to sing Gospel music. I spent most of my time in my mom's bed singing because I had so much time on my hands, those same insecurities propelled me into God's love and safety. God used these moments of praise and worship to work on my broken heart and develop a heart for Him.

God needed me to grow in loneliness so that all my hope and trust would be placed on Him. If I would have had a sister, maybe I would have been too busy playing and fighting with my sister. Instead, being an only child helped me grow closer to Him. During my alone time God would speak to me and convict me in areas of my life that needed direction. As a child I even began reading a Bible based book about Christian Morals. I wanted to do the right thing, in this book I learned the importance of respecting and loving others as I would myself. Even as a child, God was helping me build a relationship with Him and The Holy Spirit, for the ultimate calling on my life. Through the loneliness and hardships of my life God had a plan. Remember this, God knows exactly where he is taking you. Nothing is impossible for God. God used my pain and He will use your pain to draw you closer to Him. We see God's intentions in Jeremiah 11:29, "For I know the plans I have for you..." He knows exactly where he is taking you, don't worry about your pain or insecurity. If you would just trust the process, rest assured, He will blow your mind and surpass all of your expectations.

For most of my childhood I compared myself to my fellow classmates. My mom placed me and kept me in the best school in the country and that meant most of the population of kids came from a wealthy and well-off family. My mother's income could not afford me the things I saw my classmates with. Their shoes, bookbags, and transportation was far better than mine. As a child I began to believe I was less than. Everyone was better than me. I knew my mom did her best to care for me but I always felt like I didn't belong, like everyone was better than me.

Even though I had family in the United States who would help my mom financially every so often, my mom would use the extra money to pay bills and catch up on expenses. Fulfilling my wants was the least of my mother's concern. As a child I always believed my life would have been better with a father. If only my dad would have been around, then I would have had the nice shoes, the nice backpack, and a nicer house for my friends to visit. Finances would have been better for my mom with a husband by her side. Instead I grew up without a father, with a struggling mother, and watching my friends' parents pick them up in private cars while I used public transportation. Once again, in my mind, my friends were better than me. For sure I believed if my mom would only drive me to and from school I would feel "better" but boy was I wrong. It took my mother a long time before she learned how to drive. When she finally got a car, learning how to drive was yet again another obstacle. My mother was motivated by fear, she was afraid of the unknown and loved her comfort zone but things had to change. When she finally drove, she made a 30minute commute into an hour and a half journey! She drove too slow, pressed on the breaks too often, and would let all the cars past her. I used to get so frustrated and sad to see all the struggles that my mother had to go through. But my frustration and sadness stirred something in me that I did not know I had. As a child I always wanted my father's presence. I believed, if my dad would have been present my mom would have had an easier means to providing. Ultimately, I would have grown with confidence. Our living situation would have been of better quality. Without a father I grew up thinking that I was less than, I always felt like I had to do something to validate myself. Thankfully, God has a way of bringing you out of hard things and into new strength. God's plans are to prosper you not to kill you. Growing up, I bottled up many questions, which created a hole in my heart that only God was able to fill. As I grew older, I understood that what doesn't kill me, only makes me stronger.

The absence of my father developed a hardening of my heart. I wanted my father but I was complete without him, but was I really? My confusion turned into feelings of rejection and abandonment. I was angry, I didn't understand how my father could abandon me and not make an attempt to reconcile time lost.

I have only seen my father twice before the age of 27 and spoken to him over the phone a couple of times over the years, nothing consistent. Although we have a relationship, I understand now that God was designing my life the way it was because of the particular calling on my life, but as a child I did not understand his plans. Living without a father was hard and painful. Watching my friends with their fathers hurt, but as time passed the pain became more bearable until I became numb to my own feelings of abandonment. I grew up telling myself I didn't need a father. I began to tell myself my mom was more than enough. After all, she was the one providing for my needs. Isn't it funny how even at a young age, a child is able to learn how to pretend? We develop coping mechanisms without the help of anyone. It didn't help that my mother was silent to the abandonment. I knew she was just as hurt as I was but somehow we believed ignoring it would help the pain go away.

I never put my emotions into words but I definitely used anger and frustration to express my feelings. I used to throw many temper-tantrums, I screamed, I yelled, I got upset for no reason, and my all time favorite - talking back, I was a pro at that. I was always on the defense. People always asked if I was ok... I wasn't. But I made sure I always said I was. Unfortunately, my face did not match the words coming out of my mouth. The anger and frustration I felt was simply too deep. I began putting all my time and energy into dance. Dancing was my escape, I loved dancing. I remember hosting dance parties in my home with all my friends. We developed choreographies and conducted "Dance Shows." It was the best. During those dancing sessions I didn't have to think about my pain. I could be me. I could dance the pain away. Dancing allowed me to express myself without anyone knowing the pain inside. Many times, we believe God is only present when things are going well, when pain is not present. In fact, God is most present during our trials and tribulations. God used those moments of pain and uncertainty to help me and my mom become better individuals. God gave my mom strength to keep going even though it was not easy. He covered me with his love and protection because He had a purpose for my life.

Pain cannot keep you away from God's plan for your life. God uses our pain to teach others, to give them hope. We go through hardship for future generations, to help others who are going through similar situations. Have you ever encountered a difficult person? Think about it, that person did not just wake up with that personality. Life's unspoken pain and hardships resurface when not taken care of. As we grow older the wounds grow deeper. The devil uses our pain and insecurity to destroy us. The devil is able to plant deeper lies and deceptions because we are in such a vulnerable state. Our pain blinds us, our silence becomes the deadliest weapon against us. The devil is constantly at work to destroy you, he didn't just begin now. The devil has been trying to take you out since the day of your conception. Thankfully, we have a Great and Mighty God. God our great redeemer will use the pain the devil tried to destroy us with and bless us in it. Why do you think the devil is fighting so hard to take you out? Why is he making your life a living nightmare? I'll tell you why, because he knows who you are! The devil knows who God has called you to be. Once you begin to live within the call you become a dangerous threat to the forces of evil. The devil may have tried to sabotage you by using pain, rejection, betrayal and every bad thing possible to prevent you from reaching your destiny. But even then, his tactics won't work. We have a God that can change any situation and work through any situation. The only thing that may prevent God from intervening in your situation is YOU. God can heal you from any childhood pain that you may have experienced, if you would just let him.

I didn't believe I had forgiveness in my heart for my father but God made a way. Today I still have the memories of my childhood, but the memories do not cause me pain. Nor do I hold anger or resentment. I understand that my dad was not at fault, the circumstances I lived through helped me become the person I am today. If God allowed it to happen then He will use it for his glory. Think about it, why did

God allow Jesus the king of kings to be born in a manger? Mary and Joseph, his earthly parents had to go through many hardships to bring him into this world. God could have chosen the most luxurious place of birth for Jesus, but God chose a manger amongst livestock. Sometimes God will allow situations to occur to develop your character into His. Often, we are afraid to go through tough times but it is only then that we get to know who God is. God's greatest desire is for us to know who He is. In order to know who He is, you have to allow God to walk you through the good and the bad. God wants to teach you. He wants to show you who YOU have been called to be and whom you are serving.

As young as I was, the situations I have had to endure have shaped me into who I am today. Today I am patient and grateful. I may not have had everything I wanted, but I had just what I needed. God knew the environment I needed to grow up in. That environment helped me become who I am today, now I can encourage and share what I have endured with others. Through my trials and tribulations, I can now bring glory to God.

My Adolescence

I don't know about you, but my teenage years were the toughest ones yet. As a teenager you're discovering who you are and where you fit in the world. I still didn't know where I belonged. I dealt with rejection, abandonment, betrayal, embarrassment, shame, loneliness and so much more. The pain just wouldn't go away. Most of the time I felt unlucky, nothing good would ever come my way. To add to my pain at 13 years old I got left back a grade. I had to repeat my school year all over again. I was saddened because I wouldn't move forward with my friendships and ashamed for letting my mom down. In Haiti, education is very valuable, therefore repeating a grade level is very frowned upon. My mom could have taken my school grades elsewhere and I would have had the chance to move forward to the next grade level, but my mom knew I had to learn my lesson and push forward. Very quickly I developed a tough skin and learned to walk fearlessly. As time went by my fellow classmates forgot about my downfall and my situation became more bearable. I didn't understand then, but I needed to walk through the shame and embarrassment. Only then would I reach where God was taking me.

God has predestined a path for us, a path of purpose and joy. We just have to trust Him and allow Him to bring us to where only He can. Through the curves and edges, rain or shine, our trust must be placed on Him. When we learn to trust God in the midst of our pain then we'll be able to trust Him in the midst of our joy. We won't fully know the power and grace of God if we only experience the good, we must also experience moments where all of our trust must be placed in Him. I can say this now, but as a teenager I didn't understand the love and guidance of the Father. Now I know He was preparing me for who I am today. My childhood pain allowed me to gracefully enter into my adolescence. God's way may not seem like the easiest way but it is a purposeful one. The one who will take you to your destiny. Every experience, helped me become humble and appreciative even though I kept experiencing pain. I knew the pain would not be in vain. At times I felt unlucky and questioned my entire existence, but even then, I knew there had to be a better side to all of this. One day I would be able to reap a harvest of blessings.

Can you imagine turning 18 years old and not being interested in anything? Turning 18 is every child's dream come true! At 18 you are dreaming big and excited for adulthood. I was not. I was once again a mess! You may be thinking, "Can this girl catch a break?" I know. I asked myself that question all the time. A couple of weeks before my 18th birthday, I lost a friend. The only friend I ever had, had passed away unexpectedly. Finally, I felt like I had a sister, I had a friend, and now she was gone. Our friendship was unconditional. I knew I could rely on her. We did many things together, one of course was talk for hours! We knew each other so well. People even thought we were twin sisters! She was my best friend. Losing her felt horrible and unbearable. Every time I passed by her house I was reminded of the friend I had lost. What had I done to deserve this? Life was unfair but even then I had to fake a smile. I didn't think I would ever be myself again. But God had a plan for me. What burden is too heavy for God to carry? What is impossible to him? Absolutely nothing!

I know God is real because He has brought me out of darkness and into the light. He sent me not one but several other friends who I became very close with after the loss of my dear friend. One friend in particular was Liz, she was there for me through it all. Liz' family embraced me during a time of pain and hardship. Liz reminded me a lot of my friend who I had lost. I'm so thankful for the friendship Liz provided. Once again, God was bringing together his own plans. God began to bring me out of the situation I was in. Just when you think there is no way out God always shows up. There is no challenge too big for God to care for. When you let God be God, miracles will take place. In our most difficult times, that's when God becomes so much more real to us. The loss of my friend proved God's faithfulness and my ability to handle it through my faith and relationship with God. God won't let you go through trials without his direction. There is nothing that you can't handle when God is by your side. God knew I could handle this loss, He helped me through it. I don't know what obstacle or situation you are facing today but He is equipping you for your growth and destiny. In 2 Corinthians 12:9 the Bible tells us, "My grace is sufficient for you, for my power is made perfect in weakness." We are not meant to solve or carry our own problems. Instead, our job is to let God lead the way and trust in Him. Once we hand it over to God, we don't have to even think about it. I know it is not easy to remain calm in the midst of trouble, however you must train yourself to rely on God in good and bad times.

Unfortunately, I haven't always given God control over my situations. Most of the time we try to work things out on our own. Sometimes we cling to the wrong form of solution, some of us cling to drugs, alcohol, seclusion which then can form into depression, and even seeking advice from others rather than seeking guidance from God. Only God can show you how to deal with things that are too big for you to deal with. In my experience with life's trials, I would always call my friend or tried to resolve it on my own, and each time I would be left disappointed. Every time you take matters into your own hands, you will end up disappointed. I used to complain that no one was ever around to help me during my time of need when in reality, God was closing every door so that instead I would run to Him. I used to think I was unlucky, but in fact it was God's hand over my life. What I saw as "un-luck" was actually building me up for who I was called to be, everything around me was building me up to be the strong woman I am today. It took me a long time to realize this, I had to learn the hard way. But I learned if you find yourself dealing with betrayals and rejections, you need to pause for a moment and ask God why. Just like you, I did not understand all the trials in my life until God explained it to me. Once God revealed it to me everything made sense and I became at ease with myself and the journey ahead. I understood who I was in God and accepted my identity In God.

When we rely on friends or family then God is not who He is supposed to be in our life; your friends or family take the place of God. It is good to have friends and family but they are not to take God's place. If for every trial your friends are the first ones whom you call, then you are looking for your friendships to help you resolve your situation. Now, it is true that God may send a friend to help you but the goal is for you not to rely on your friend for every trial. The goal is to rely on God. Our first cry for help should be to God never on our own understanding because sometimes we may put ourselves in a situation where we cannot get out of. God is very jealous and doesn't want it this way. That is why it is so important that we have a personal relationship with our creator so that we may know who He is. The Bible says in Jeremiah 17:7, "But blessed is the one who trusts in the Lord, whose confidence is in him." The Bible also says in Jeremiah 17:5, "Cursed is the one who trusts in man, who draws strength from mere flesh and whose heart turns away from the Lord." It is good to have friends or family who support us, who are there when we need them because we were created to get along with one another and to love one another. But it is not ok to put them before God. Putting God first is not easy because as humans we are so used to seeing things with our natural eyes therefore it is not easy to put God first and trust when we cannot see Him. It is easy to believe or trust your mom for example because you can see her, when you talk to her she answers, or when something goes wrong she is there to comfort. But trusting God will require a whole different level of approach. No one was born with the ability to trust God. It took me years of deception, revelation, trials, and tribulations to trust God. Experiences will help you place your trust in God, it will take time but keep trusting. Sometimes, it takes being alone and things to "fall into place" for you to realize that God had it all under control. You learn that when your trust is placed in God he never leaves you or forsakes you (Deuteronomy 31:6). It's not easy to place your trust in God from one day to the next, but start small and you'll see your faith and trust grow in Him. Remember He created you for a purpose! The calling on your life requires your trust in God. You have to trust God with all your heart because you are called to lead by example and help others to see God through you.

Many times, we have to go through deceptions, rejections, or even painful situations where we may think that people are against us but in reality God is pushing us to our calling and purpose. If you seek dependence on friends, family or even yourself, you are going to miss the voice of God, you may even miss the calling on your life. Growing up I saw my mom pray religiously, she always spoke about who God was. We attended church and practiced "waiting on God." But I had to know God for myself. You shouldn't serve God through someone else's faith or obedience, when you begin to know God from a personal level you begin to serve wholeheartedly. When I was a kid, I used to pray because I had to, it was a routine. But as I got older,

I realized who God was and developed my own relationship with him. I evolved from routinely seeking him to seeking him because I desired to. My experiences led me to spending time with God, I couldn't do life the same anymore. I needed more of His love and guidance. At 35 years old, I continue to experience who God is in my everyday life. I encourage you to do the same. Don't stop seeking his voice, love, and guidance. The more time you spend with God the more you will grow to love him. For instance, I love my husband and I get to learn more about my husband as the days go by, as we spent time together. The more I spend time with him, the more I love him. Even through the very tough times in marriage, I still love him and trust in our future together. Tough trials have made us stronger as a team, as we endure we grow and become better for one another. Our relationship with God runs the same. Trials cannot separate us, it only builds more strength between us. I trust God, I know God is for me. If He is there for me, He is most definitely there for you.

During trying times, our emotions change, our circumstances change but God never does. God is constant and withstanding, he is always by your side even when you can't see or hear him. Many of us only seek God when we want a miracle or a selfish desire. But when times get tough, instead of seeking God we begin to walk away from him. Unfortunately, sometimes we think bad circumstances are a reflection of God's un-love for us or much worse that God is nonexistent. I used to think that God didn't love me because I was always facing trials and tribulations. Ironically, God knew those circumstances would bring me closer to him. I needed to realize that without God I was lost, I needed God during those times to teach me and show me the way. If we could just be patient, we would be able to see his hand over our lives. No situation is ever too big or too small for God. God is for us not against us. As soon as we realize whose we are our lives would take a happier course. Our trust in God will take us places we never ever imagined, just give it a try! Be patient, draw near, and trust God!

My Adult Years

In July 2003, I made a decision that changed my life forever. With the help of my cousin, Jenn I moved to The United States of America. Though my mother did not agree with the move, I knew it was the best decision for me. I was excited for the fresh start and ability to change the course of my life. I knew that The United States was different from Haiti, but what I didn't know was the speed in which I would begin "adulting." My mother was no longer around to guide and support me, for the first time I had to take full control of my life. Thankfully, my aunt and cousins who lived in The United States provided their support and I am thankful for each and every one of them. Even with all the help provided, it became difficult for everyone to offer their help. Life in The United States is a constant "Go, Go, Don't stop" kind of mentality and I realized I had a lot of catching up to do, especially if I was going to make it out with grace. Everything I had experienced in my past helped me move forward to my future. God knew that I needed the training back home because of the life that was waiting for me in The United States. Trusting God with all of our detours is the most gratifying choice, because God knows best. He knows our next step and the best way to go about it. I know that now, but I surely did not know that then. If I did, I would have avoided many mistakes, many heartaches, and many more headaches.

I did not know how important it was to know the voice of God and most importantly how to follow it. It is only when I became a born again Christian that I understood many things. In my youth, I believed if I simply prayed and believed that God was all powerful that life would be great. I believed in God but I did whatever I wanted. I would pray for one thing and would do the complete opposite without consulting God. Then I would reap my consequences and cry to Him whenever my options did not work out. My heart wanted to do the right thing but my will would always take over. I had a one-way relationship with God. I could tell God what to do but God couldn't tell me what to do. I was walking on water and drowning! Many of us are still drowning. Making an attendance on Sunday, doing all Sunday-Funday stuff, and forgetting to follow through with the voice of God. God is above everything in this world, He created everything. Nobody knows better than God. God is the best consultant there could ever be. He has the key for your success and your happiness. Whatever makes you happy, God can give it. Many of us are thankful for all that God has done in our lives. We know that God is great and above all but we don't invite God into our everyday life. Like I said, I had a one-way relationship with God. I was ignoring the fact that God actually wanted to be involved in every detail of my life, as with yours. God wants to help you in the small and big, in the happy and sad, God wants to be involved. When we place God in the center of our lives, we begin to live a life with purpose.

I must confess, I did not have God in the center of my life before. But now that I put God first, my life has a meaning and I am living my best life.

You cannot live your best life by yourself because there are too many things in life against you. In Matthew 6:33 NLT we read, "Seek the kingdom of God above all else, and live righteously, and he will give you everything you need." Seek God before you seek for your career or your spouse and do the right thing, listen to the direction of God, and he will provide the desires of your heart. God loves you, his mercy is shed upon you every morning. Trust and obey when He speaks. Don't waste time, stop taking detours, walk in your calling, in your promise. Only you can take the next step. God already loves and cares for you. Lamentations 3:22-23 says, "Because of the Lord's great love we are not consumed, for his compassion never fails. They are new every morning; great is your faithfulness."

So I moved to The United States to pursue a better life. Before moving forward with a job or school I had to wait on legal documents stating my residency. What began as an exciting adventure became a long dreaded disappointment. Reality was setting in very quickly. Frustration, regret, and doubt began to take place instead of excitement. While I waited for the legality aspect to take place, I did not understand the work that was happening inside of me. I became responsible and hungry for success. I saw everyone around me doing something productive and I wanted to do the same. The wait made me appreciate the importance of independence and I promised myself not to take this new opportunity for granted. As soon as I was granted access to work, I took it very seriously and began working. I was no longer interested in going out to parties, my job was my priority and I was willing to work hard to get to where I wanted. I was working a crazy amount of hours as a Home Health Aid unfortunately my paycheck was not a reflection of it. But I did not let it stop me because I had a goal. After working one full year, I enrolled in school and was attending both school and work full time. The small amount of time I had for myself no longer existed but I was hungry for the success, I was going to push forward.

After attending school for a total of three semesters, I met my husband and became pregnant and my whole world turned upside down. Pregnancy was complicated. I was 22 years old with no stable status in the country, no real job, no degree, I wasn't married, and I barely knew my husband at that time. So many reasons as to why I should not continue with the pregnancy. I had never been so scared and confused. My biggest fear was to face my mother who did not want me to move here in the first place. The thought of her being disappointed was killing me. Pregnancy was the hardest decision I had to make and the odds were against me. After careful deliberation, I decided to continue with the pregnancy and trust God. After I made the decision, so many people walked out on me. Not only was it a hard pregnancy physically, pregnancy took an emotional toll on me. I had to face shame and loneliness. It was hard and stressful. Instead of being happy and excited for my first born, I was scared and confused. My mom was in Haiti and I felt alone. I didn't feel like I had a support system I could run to.

From time to time, I would find someone who would do something for me but it was a lonely walk most of the time. Towards the end of my pregnancy, I moved out of my aunts house, and began renting a room from someone; a room not an apartment. Things were just going from bad to worse and there was no one to put a stop to it. But I remembered, God was a fair God, He wouldn't give me anything I couldn't handle. If you are going through something hard and you feel like you can't handle it, you are right. You can't handle it on your own. You need God. God doesn't put you through something without equipping you for it. Your past lessons have a purpose to build your strength for new challenges. Your past challenges are like bridges to help you handle your new ones. Without challenges there is no growth. People who are comfortable and stay stagnant in one situation are not allowing themselves to grow. Like I said, God prepares you for what is coming your way. You might not see it or feel it but as you go on with life, each challenge built you for the next one. Remember that a life without challenges is a life without growth. If I would have never experienced rejection, betrayal or loneliness, it would have been harder for me to face it when I was pregnant with my child. All of those hard experiences were a prerequisite for what was waiting for me when I moved to The United States.

By the grace of God, I went through with the pregnancy and decided to trust God no matter what came my way. Trusting God through the process was very hard and draining because of the amount of humiliation that I had to endure. But God gave me the grace to stick to the plan which was to bring life to my daughter. In the midst of trusting God, it will require a lot of death to self. Many times, you will have to let people talk, laugh, or even mock you because the plan of God doesn't often make sense. Just like when Noah was building the ark, everyone was laughing at him until it started raining. Like Noah, my faith and trust were grounded in who God was. I had to make a conscious decision to put my situation in God's hands. Only God could make the best of my worst. The grace and mercy of God is something we will never be able to comprehend. Regardless of all the mistakes and the time God had to put into making my wrongs right, He still showed me grace and an unending love. As long as you trust God in a situation, you will never be disappointed.

After a long and overdue pregnancy, I gave birth to the most beautiful baby girl. I thank God for my child. But once again, I received a very quick reality check. It was not easy to take care of a baby. I was on my own and with no help. From time to time someone would stop by but I was taking care of my daughter on my own. It was extremely hard and draining not only because I was new to motherhood but also because I did not have a support system. After one month of motherhood, my mother came to visit for a month and towards the end of her visit we decided the best next step was for my daughter to return to Haiti with my mom. In the meantime, I would get myself in a better financial position to take care of my daughter. It was a pretty hard decision but it had to be done. Thinking of it right now, I would not be able to send my two-month old to the nearest state let alone another country! But God gave me the strength and grace to do so. I'm glad I did, it was the best decision at that time.

In my opinion, mothers are the next best thing after God. I am forever grateful for my mother. While my daughter was in Haiti, I was very focused to make the best of the situation. I went from being a Home Health Aid to a Certified Nursing Assistant. I got myself a good job and was working non stop so I could be prepared for the return of my daughter. After being a Certified Nursing Assistant for a year, I enrolled in Nursing school. I worked so hard that I was able to pay for school tuition on my own. While I was going to school, my husband who was at the time my boyfriend supported me and I was able to graduate with my License Practical Nurse certification. It may seem easy reading through the description of my journey of becoming a nurse, getting my finances in order, and aligning my life, but the journey was long and hard. My daughter was my motivation. Every time I wanted to quit she was my reminder that I needed to make it for her. She deserved the best, I had to roll back my sleeves and get to work. God had been preparing me all along for this and I needed to focus more than ever. Finally, I finished the nursing program one month before my daughter turned three years-old and she was back in my arms. All the hard work had paid off. I'm telling you, God is the best redeemer! He knows how to turn things around, how to turn your mess into a message only if you allow him to. The journey was hard but God did it!

My nursing career had given me some kind of financial stability which allowed me to take care of my daughter and have a decent life. However, I was not satisfied. I was hungry for more success. I had a feeling there was more, I had more levels to achieve. I was starving for more success. I came from a family where people worked hard. Every single person in my family had worked hard for their success. It was in my DNA, working hard was not an issue for me. With little sleep, I began to work up to 16 hours a day, even more sometimes. I began to work several jobs to create a secure financial life for me and my family. I developed a strong work ethic and after a few years I was able to purchase a house. By that time, I had my second daughter, and married while carrying my son. God had really showed me grace for someone who started off on a rough path. When you allow God to take over, he works the best into your life. What started off as bad can finish off as beautiful. If you would have told me that my story would end up that way, I would have never believed it. In the humblest way I say this, I know many people who have had a great support system and yet things have not taken a good turn. The most common question is Why? And I truly believe the answer behind my success is all thanks to God. Had I not trusted God, my story would have been so much different. I trusted God from the beginning, he showed up and turned my situation around. Throughout the years, God always blessed me with great employment opportunities. God always left an open door for me. God turned all my trials into testimonies and I am forever grateful for that. Placing my trust in God has been the best decision I've ever made.

Many times, trusting God means we follow God's voice and we do what may not make the most sense to us or anyone else. Trusting God means we do things God's way. In my case, I chose to carry and provide for my baby despite all the odds that were against me. There is nothing that you do for God that will go unnoticed. Whatever you do in private for him, He will reward you in public. "He is a rewarder of those who diligently seek him" Hebrews 11:6 NKJV. Every time you make a decision and include God in it, he will work it in a way that no one can. Even if you don't have a close relationship with him, His love for you is bigger than anything. God is patiently waiting for any occasion that you may call on his name to show you how much he loves you! Take it from me, I was not supposed to be where I am today but God will prove your enemies wrong every time you decide to let him in on the battle; God will fight for you and He will always win! God had a plan for me all along even when I did not have one for myself. God is the only one who can modify, add, remove, or erase things from your life whenever he wants. No matter how broken you are, give the pieces to God and trust him. He's done it for me, so he will do it for you! Each and every time your trust will grow, because his love never fails.

Miraculous things happen when your trust is placed in God and you follow through with obedience. Through my obedience in God, I was able to break a generational curse! You may be asking, "What is a generational curse? or "How do I break a generational curse?" Let me explain, generational curses are continuous obstacles that are passed on from one generation to the next in a family blood line to prevent people from reaching their purpose or destiny. Lamentations 5:7 KJV states, "Our fathers have sinned, and are not; and we have borne their iniquities." Generational curses can exist at the financial, health, and social level. Sometimes a family can struggle with several curses at once. God always chooses someone in the family to break the generational curse and path a way for new journeys.

In my case, most women in my family have not taken the step to marry, to establish a covenant in marriage. I on the other hand took our family to the next level! Most of the women in my mother's side are not married. Even though I started off as pregnant and not married, God made a way for me to marry the father of my children. As a woman, I grew up with no knowledge or example of what "marriage" entailed. Getting married, being able to find someone who I could do life with was a huge spiritual accomplishment. When a generational curse is broken and goes against the "common" history, it opens doors for future generations to walk through. In my case, I have opened the door for marriages to take place for the men and women of my family. I was able to set the standard for others to follow along. So, who can break a generational curse? Anyone whom God has chosen. God designates who he wants for such a task. There is no specific requirement. For instance, Joseph was a chosen one. Chosen to bring forth God's divine plan. Joseph suffered and endured the challenges at hand, Joseph developed the traits and the heart needed to carry out God's plan. Like Joseph, we too need to suffer and endure, this will make us stronger for the battle and the victory! Joseph endured betrayal, abandonment, and so much more, Joseph was being prepared. God has chosen you for the task. The challenges will only bring you closer to God. Whatever challenge is at hand in your life today, you will overcome because God stands beside you.

Rely on God, trust in God, and remember he is your best friend. Family and friends will tend to let you down, not God. In my experience, no friendship can give me what God has. From the moment I let God in and took him as a friend, everything had a different perspective. He gives the best advice, strategy, and he tells the truth. Place all your relationships in God's hand first, He will keep or remove whatever relationships you need to help you in your journey. I am confident that my relationships and experiences will bring honor and glory to God, because he is fully in charge. My trust in God is undeniably the force that pushes me forward into my calling. When you place God first, everything else finds its way into your blessing. Rest in God and know he is for you, never against you. Take charge, you can open the next door for your family to walk through!

Understanding God's Call

Have you ever felt like a working machine? A machine that never stops? That was me. With three kids, a working husband, and bills, money just wasn't ever enough. Bills kept piling up, our home needed attention, and our budget was out on a tangent. There just wasn't enough hours in the day for all of life's responsibilities. I felt like I was running in circles! We hired a nanny and eventually I even took on up to three jobs, and that was still not enough! How on earth? Things would always come up to throw our savings off, from bills, to our car breaking down, or unseen home expenses… Life was really playing with our money. The worst part of all of this was the time lost with our children. It was hard and I could not understand what was going on. My mind was constantly working, trying to come up with new ideas to bring more income. I thought I was going to lose it, my finances were simply not making any sense. What I had not realized was my lack of communication with God about the jobs I was taking on. I thought that as a believer and child of God, that he would simply bless whatever job I took, that was definitely not the case. This is a very common mistake. We take on jobs, relationships, and so much more without ever consulting God. Many of us go on in life making very important decisions without involving God and then we wonder why we fail or are so unhappy or frustrated. Here is why- we haven't consulted with God first. God created us and knows exactly which path we should take, so why not ask God for guidance first? God knows who we should marry, what career path we should take or what business venture we should sign up for. After all, He knows everything about us, before we were even born he created us in our mother's womb. Jeremiah 29:11 states, "For I know the plans I have for you," declares the LORD, "plans to prosper you and not to harm you, plans to give you hope and a future." Trust God and ask him what your next step should be, follow the call placed in your life.

Imagine all the time saved if we would talk to God, hear his direction and follow it. Sometimes life's distractions hinder our one on one with God and we miss his voice. When we miss God's voice, we end up wasting time, losing money, struggling in relationships, and missing sleep! God's voice will always direct you into your destiny and calling. Your calling is your purpose, the reason you have been placed on this planet. The reason he created you. Real fulfillment always comes from operating in your purpose. People usually get "career" and "calling" confused, because we've been so heavily programmed to focus on our career, but in reality, your calling is your purpose not your job. Although you career can be a bridge to your purpose, ultimately you have been designed to prosper in your purpose.

Often times we dismiss our purpose, we dismiss the passion and skill set inside of us. For example, ever since I was a little girl, I had a passion to help people. As I got older the passion grew and grew! I remember volunteering and being so excited to share the opportunity to help those in need. God created me that way. I like to motivate people, I like to advise people on making better decisions to improve their life, that is my purpose in life. God called me to help others, push people, motivate, convince, encourage, and give hope. That is my purpose. Because I have seen God turn my life around, it is easier for me to see and tell someone God can also turn their life around. What may seem impossible to you is surely possible for God.

After seven years in nursing, I came into the realization that maybe nursing was simply not for me, not long term at least. It was the right decision for the season, but ultimately it became a financial burden as time went by. Even after earning a license in Nursing and working years in it, I felt empty inside, I felt like there was so much I could do, I just didn't know what, when, or how. Regardless of what route you take, whether you let God in or not, He will always steer you back into your purpose. I wanted to fill my void so badly that I actually returned to Nursing school to continue with my education. I was putting myself in more debt, but that's what we do when we are outside of God's will! As I continued on this path, I believed it would be a breeze... but it wasn't. My science and nursing classes became more stressful and harder to complete. I ended up failing a science class and I thought of quitting, but I didn't. And then my mom got sick, my nanny quit on me, and I even lost some friendships. Caring for my mom in her time of sickness became very hard, it required many trips to the hospital and on top of that I had the children, work, school, and life to manage. Thankfully, by God's grace I was able to finish the semester. Even though I was outside of God's will he was still merciful towards me. God's grace and mercy don't make sense; no matter what we do we will never understand it.

One December day, as I was leaving school to go home in between classes to check on my mother and my son, I heard a voice, it was loud and clear. There was no way I could have missed that voice. The voice of God said to me: "I did not call you for Nursing." For a moment, I did not understand what was happening. I knew it wasn't my own voice or thought. Afterall, nursing was e-ver-ry-thing to me!

I believed pursuing Nursing would fulfill me, but deep down, I was simply taking matters into my own hands instead of letting God guide me. I was sure I had heard God's voice, and I'm glad he spoke. I finally felt at ease because I knew what I was not supposed to pursue. It felt like a weight had been lifted off my shoulders, I was relieved and content for God's revelation in my life. Reading and knowing what the Bible has to say is an excellent way to help us walk with God, spending time with God allows us to hear from him, so that when he finally speaks we are able to recognize his voice. Keep in mind, God's revelations never expire. God's revelations are like passes that we find along our journey that tell us about the next destination. So every single one of them is important because it is the key for the next door. God's revelations are a lamp unto our feet to the way and the truth. So how do we hear from God? We spend time with him. It is important to spend time with God so that we may hear from him, without his voice and direction we may end up lost or full of worry.

There are so many directions and pathways our lives can take if we are not careful, the enemy can lure us into places and space we were never meant to be. Without God's guidance, we may end up in the wrong places. Look at it like this, a person who cannot hear from God cannot receive revelation, therefore he or she is like a car without head lights. A car without headlights runs with danger, within any minute the car may steer the wrong way or crash while in darkness. Are you a running car without headlights? Are you walking in darkness without the voice of God? Take some time to spend with God. He will guide you and protect you into your destiny.

After I heard God's voice I ran into many questions. I began to doubt whether putting Nursing school down would be beneficial for me and my family. I knew I didn't want to continue Nursing school, but how else would I fulfill the emptiness inside? Notice here that all along I was trying to fulfill my emptiness. When in reality, God was trying to fill all the areas in my life that needed filling. Nursing school was the easiest option for me when I came to The United States, I knew I wanted to help people so where else but to begin a career in Nursing? I'm grateful for what I've learned in Nursing school, but deep down it didn't make me happy. I knew there was more to life. I just didn't know what or how to get there. Keep in mind that no matter how much money you make, if you are not happy it is not worth it. Happiness is more important than money. Purpose is more important than money.

During my years in Nursing, I learned that your career or job will drain you but your purpose will fulfill you. I'm glad that God opened my eyes and brought me to my purpose. From time to time I miss going to school for Nursing and think about how far I could have been but God's way is the best way and I trust him with everything. Although I could not discern the voice of God in the past, I see now all the roadblocks and closed doors He used to align my purpose. Once upon a time I remember receiving a vision from God. In this vision, I had a microphone in my hand. I didn't understand the vision, but now I know God was calling me to something much greater than myself. I was too busy then to understand God's vision for me, but today I have zero regrets for leaving Nursing School. In all honesty, I did not think obeying God would feel so good. Even though I don't know my next step concerning school, it feels great to rely solely on God and not my own motives or understanding. I am relying completely on God to guide me and show me what's next. Giving God full control of one's life is not an easy thing to do but it is the best thing. Trusting God can sometimes become upsetting because God doesn't tell us every detail of what he is doing while we are waiting. But God knows best! Give Him control.

Many times, we may feel like time is running out or we're being unproductive during the wait, but God will never let you down. God loves you and will show you again and again the benefits of trusting in him. It wasn't always easy for me to trust God but as I made room for God to move in my life, I knew his ways would always blow me away. I have learned that the more I trust in God, the more he is able to do and the less I have to worry. Writing about giving God my trust is easier said than done. It has taken some falls but a great amount of faith to execute God's orders in my life. Following God's voice into obedience is not an easy task, it requires that you do things that you don't understand or cannot see. As humans, we have to see before we believe. Whereas in the spiritual, we have to believe before we can see. We walk by faith and not by sight (2 Corinthians 5:7). Sometimes our walk will feel lonely, our faith walk may not make sense to those around us, but God's word must ring true in our hearts. God will not leave us nor forsake us (Deuteronomy 31:6).

God wants us to rely only on him because only then will our faith begins to grow and expand to new spaces. Those who once thought our walk seemed irrational will be able to see the victory in walking by faith and not by sight. Our faith can and will become contagious. Nevertheless, sometimes even people who share the same beliefs as we do may not understand what God is doing in your life, and that's ok! God's ways are not our ways. Don't be discouraged by the questioning of those around you, trust that God has your best interest. Not everyone will understand your walk or the calling God has placed in your life, because that call is on your life, not theirs. Walk in obedience, stay the course, read the word of God and trust that God will place the right people along the way for you.

If you are struggling with your purpose, or not sure if you are operating in the right field or your intuition is telling you that there is more to life, the only way to find out your next step is to ask God! The Bible says, "My people are destroyed from lack of knowledge." Hosea 4:6 KJV Therefore, seek knowledge, ask God for guidance. Build a relationship with God and be willing to receive instruction for him. Where He leads he will provide. People are imperfect and will always try to steer you away from God's will, so be careful who you surround yourself with. Be intentional about your relationship with God so that all your trust may be placed in him. If God instructs you to leave or begin a new endeavor, do it. Trust that God has something greater for you. As soon as you become willing to sound or look like a fool for God, he will begin to use you and show you new dreams and visions for your life. As I mentioned before, obedience and trust in God does not come easy to most but God will give you strength for every day that you walk in his will. Take a step forward, God is for you.

I Said "Yes" to God

In 2018 my life became clearer. Life finally made sense. I finally knew who I was in God. I realized I had been chosen by God. I had all the answers to all my questions. At last, I understood why I had to go through betrayal, loneliness, misunderstanding, and so much more. Everything made sense and I was at peace with my new identity in Christ. I knew I had changed. I was different and that was ok. When you are chosen by God, there is no need to compare yourself to others because you are not like others. People will notice the change in you, some will want to take advantage of you, others will become jealous of you, some won't know how to appreciate your change and reject you. But keep your eyes on God, he will hold you and sustain you through all the changes around you and in you. Again, it is not easy but you must continue your journey towards your purpose.

When you look in the mirror, do you know who you are? Are you aware of the calling God has placed in your life? You might not know who you are right now, sometimes life's circumstances help you figure out who you've been called to be. In other cases, if you take the time you can begin to put the pieces together. Think about it, deep down you have dreams and aspirations that bring you life! Are you purposely ignoring who you are? Are you scared or clueless about how to get to your purpose? I've been there. Don't ignore who you've been called to be. Trust in God, he has the best prepared for you. But if you don't answer the call, if you continue postponing it, either way, God will create scenarios until you fully surrender to your calling. I kept running away from my calling, I thought I was on the right path. I was working hard to create the best life for myself and my family. But even all the hours worked in my three jobs was never enough to pay my bills. How could that even be possible you may ask. I remember asking myself the same exact question. I was living in disobedience, running away from God and running to myself for all the answers. My home was a big chaos and it was my fault because I was not where I needed to be. When we disobey God, we can cause our whole family to suffer! Can you imagine your kids suffering because of your disobedience? King David also made the same mistake, his disobedience caused many Israelites to die (2 Samuel 24:11-13).

When I look back, I can see all my mistakes. I see the hours that turned into days that I missed out from being with my children due to my multiple jobs. I used to call the shots, I did everything on my own strength, when all God ever wanted was for his power to be made perfect in my weakness (2 Corinthians 12:9). After so many years of pain and mistakes, I repented and admitted that I was a big mess and the more I tried to fix things the more I drowned. In 2018, I spent the whole year learning how to surrender to God, how to rely on him, and how to obey his voice. It was like being back in Kindergarten, I was relearning life. I had to throw away my old ways and let God take over for me. I was giving God full control of my life. In other words, I no longer had an opinion or say in my life, I was from now on, a servant to God my Lord!

Surrendering was not easy. That year was the hardest but the most rewarding. I had a lot of changing to do but God knew I would be equipped for the work ahead. Please remember that as powerful as God truly is, he can't begin a work in you without your permission first; he needs the ok from you to begin. The more time I spent with God, the more I wanted to be with him. His presence was beautiful, as time went by I knew he was doing a new work in me. I encourage you to spend time with God, you won't regret it. He will fill you and replace your sadness with peace and joy. Give him access, trust the process. My husband usually asks why I'm still awake at night, but what he doesn't understand is that I feel the closest to God when I am on my knees. My husband thinks there is something wrong with me but he just doesn't understand it yet. I remember my years attending church and praying but never experiencing the presence of God. I think it is imperative that people get to experience the presence of God through relationship. Once you experience it, your life will never be the same. The presence of God fills you with everything you may need, joy, peace, strength, emotional and physical healing, wisdom, patience, understanding and so much more. You'll notice that when you are in the presence of God you forget about all your worries. All the bills that are due or the hurt you experienced are forgotten. You are so focused on how good God is that you can't do anything else but to honor him and praise his name. I urge you to pursue the presence of God, you won't ever be the same. Jeremiah 29:13 says, "You will seek me and find me when you seek me with all your heart." Don't look for God in the wrong places like I used to do. Look for Him with your heart and where ever you are, you will be able to experience the presence of God. You don't have to be in a Church to experience the presence of God, it could be in your room, the bathroom, your office, or in a park! For me personally, kneeling in front of my bed in my room is where I meet with God every morning to get instructions for the day. I can't urge you enough, make time and experience God's presence.

As soon as I said "Yes" to the call of God in my life everything began to fall in place. I began to say "Yes" to God every day. My "Yes" led to many changes in my life, God worked things out of my life and filled me with his Holy Spirit. I am also thankful to my Spiritual mentor Maureen who God used to guide me unto my calling. When we give God permission in our life, he will place the right people in our lives. All the changes and opportunities in my life were done by God and I just had to pay attention to whatever the Holy Spirit had to say. When you allow the Holy Spirit to speak and guide you, you will be convicted unto your next steps. We all need the Holy Spirit, the Holy Spirit can help you discern your actions. Most importantly, with the Holy Spirit by your side you are more aware of how your actions affect your calling. Sin is able to be kept at a distance with God's help. An area where God began to work in me was in my lying. I thought lying was ok if it meant protecting myself. But, surely, lying was not of God. God is truth and as a daughter of Christ, I had to represent my God in everything I did and said. To be honest, I loved the way the Holy Spirit began to change me. It didn't feel intrusive, it was loving and kind, graceful, firm but always gracious. I just love everything about God! God is perfect in every way.

There were three areas in my life that required more time and more attention after willingly answering the call of God. I struggled with surrendering, relying, and obeying God. For an entire year it was a struggle, the process was intense, but God never gave up on me. I am still a work in progress but I'm not where I used to be. By living in this world, we adapt to its culture, it's easy to fall back into what we know. We do things of this world which are unpleasant to God, but thankfully the Holy Spirit reminds us of who we are and the importance of our calling in the Kingdom of God. One experience or encounter with God is not enough for complete change, our life must be constantly seeking God's guidance. From time to time, I find myself going back to old ways and I realize the hindrance of distractions. A distraction can pull you in the opposite direction of God, living for God is not a done deal, a one-time thing. Living for God is a daily choice. Everyday you must choose to give your life for the call, for the kingdom, and for the many lives that depend on it. Without the Holy Spirit, we are lost. We need the Holy Spirit every single day to be better sons and daughters. Ask the Holy Spirit to take its place in your life, let it guide you and help you be everything you need to be until Jesus returns. The following are practical steps into the areas I have struggled with:

Surrender to God

Surrender to God is easy but requires several steps. In order to surrender to God, one must have a few things in order. In my personal definition, surrender to God is to leave everything concerning you to Him. To give Him full access to your life. To surrender to God is to submit to his will for your life in all aspects. You cannot say that you surrender to God and still make decisions without his approval. Before you make decisions, you must keep in mind what would God want. Consult God first, pray. Will my decision affect my relationship with God or will it affect the plan that God has for me? Even though God is powerful and can make anything happen, we should seek to do his will and not live in disobedience. We must consult God in all of our plans and wait for him to answer. We cannot surrender to God in one area of our choosing and not give him access to other areas that need work. The areas I don't submit to God will affect the ones that I have willingly surrendered to God. To surrender to God is to forget about yourself and put the focus on God. If you are still thinking about yourself, you cannot surrender to God. You must totally give God full access to every thing, he has to have first priority in everything. For example, you cannot say that you surrender to God and when someone says something bad to you- you clap back and answer harshly.

Allow the Holy Spirit to guide you as far as what to say or do. You cannot let yourself be led by emotion or by your flesh. There is a process to surrendering to God. You must first acknowledge that he is your creator and without him you are nothing. You must stay in contact with him by praying. If you don't have a prayer life, it is going to be impossible to surrender to God. And when you surrender to God, it is the Holy Spirit that is going to do the work in you. You need to make yourself available to do whatever the Holy Spirit wants to do in you. Not only will you surrender to God in good times but also in bad times because when you surrender to God you tell him "Yes" every day and in whatever circumstances that come your way. For example, when I left Nursing school, that was an act of surrender to God. I placed my control aside and gave God full control of what was next in my life.

Rely on God

After you surrender to God, you must rely on him. Relying on God means you trust him but also place all your dependence on him. Many times, we say we trust God but depend on others, that is not relying on God. That's lying. I used to pray and say "God I leave everything in your hands" but as soon as things began to look or feel unsteady, I proceed to do things on my own. I knew God could change the course of my life. I just did not rely on Him. When you rely on God, you wait on him because you know that he has your back. You don't even depend on yourself because you know that your father knows exactly what he is doing. As the Bible says in Proverbs 3:5-6, "Trust in the Lord with all your heart and lean not on your understanding; in all your ways submit to him, and he will make your paths straight." Don't trust your own understanding, trust only God because he is omnipotent. Do not lean on others because they can change anytime, God on the other hand is constant. God will never fail you. God is always in control if you give him access to your life, he might not give you what you want at the time you expect it but if it is his will, he will give it when he knows that you need it. When you rely on God, you ask God first before asking someone else. Always seek God first. Relying on God is not an easy process but if you practice patience you may hear from him, but if you don't hear from him, simply trust that he is still in control and caring for you. A great example of practicing patience in a waiting time was when God asked me to write a book. I didn't know anyone personally who had written a book, my own understanding said I was not qualified. But my God! My God said "Do it!" I relied on God and said "Yes" along the way and here we are. I no longer depend on myself. I depend on God. I don't need to understand everything because the one who I rely on knows all things.

Obey His Voice

Before someone can obey the voice of God, he has to be able to hear the voice of God. God is always talking to us but sometimes we don't know the difference. We mistake God's voice for our voice. To hear God's voice, we must spend quality time with him. The more you spend time with God, the more you know his voice and the sound of his voice. Spend time praying, reading the Bible, and worshipping him, that will help you hear the voice of God. When you are seeking God with all your heart, God will answer your request. It is the same when you are seeking God for who he is, he will reveal himself to you. When God reveals himself to you, you will get to know him on a personal level. You will hear his voice, you will know about his character, and so much more!

Find a quiet time and place to hear God. Time with God can be any time of the day. Choose 15-20 minutes to spend with God, turn off your phone and eliminate all distractions so you can hear God's voice. You can meet with God anywhere. The bathroom, your bedroom, anywhere you choose God will meet you there. I meet with God first thing in the morning because I try to put him first, it was not like that when I began meeting with God but along the way the Holy Spirit guided me on improving my quality time with God. Once you start being in God's presence, you will not want to leave his side. There is something about God's presence that will just pull you toward him. The feeling is greater than anything that I have ever experienced. Time with God is one of a kind. You can talk about everything and anything without being judged. You can lay down your burden and know that you don't ever have to worry about them anymore. Where you meet God is a secret place and no one will ever know what you talk to him about. You will always get an answer concerning what you spoke to him about. Once you know how to hear the voice of God in private, you will know when he is talking to you in public, even with as many distractions around you. There could be loud sounds and large crowds around you, and you will be able to recognize the voice of God. All thanks to your obedience during your quiet time.

After you master hearing the voice of God, you will be able to obey him. Your love for God will grow so strong that your heart will simply be willing to obey. It takes many experiences and a willing heart and faith to obey his voice. Naturally we dislike taking direction from others, we like being in control and though that is normal do your very best to obey wholeheartedly. Obeying God requires constant surrender, and to be honest sometimes I don't obey God. I hear God and begin to doubt. Like I mentioned before, I am still a work in progress. Nevertheless, when I do obey God I am never let down, I always see the promises and love of God. Obeying God's voice is really to our own advantage and the Kingdom of God. Don't turn a deaf ear, listen, lean in to what God wants to tell you and obey. Many times, we miss our breakthrough because of our disobedience. When you are obedient to God, he is able to open spiritual and materialistic doors that bless our lives.

Saying yes to God is a very tight road and requires constant self-evaluations, but it is so worth it! Say "Yes" to God every day, and take it one day at a time. Some days will be easier than others, but at the end of the day you have the Holy Spirit to guide you along the way. Keep constant communication with God, he will help you. Continue saying "Yes" to God. Even on days when you feel lost and confused, keep saying "Yes!"

My Life After I Answered

I was a different person after I answered God's call. My mindset was changing slowly and I was very excited. I never felt that way before, it felt like I could conquer the world. I was excited for my future. For a long time, I knew God's hand was over me, what I didn't know was that I had a calling. I never knew I would be working for God or that God would be the center of my life. I knew I loved God but I never imagined being so close to him. After everything I've been through all I can do is honor God with my life, I am thankful and will forever worship his goodness. The process is not easy but if you continue to stay in communication with God, he will reveal to you what areas of your life need changing. I gave God the opportunity to train me and teach me his ways. I relied on God to prune me and shape me into the woman of God I am today. As I continued on this journey with Him, he began to remove people from my life. Without the need of misunderstandings or arguments, my phone began to ring less. It was hard to see my friends being removed from my life, at times it was lonely, but I trusted God. I knew God had a plan. I had to let friends go and make Jesus my number one friend. As I spent more time with God, I began to read my bible and pray more than before. My prayers were not scheduled or part of my "routine", my prayers were simply conversations with God. I didn't want to see my relationship with God as something boring or mandatory, I wanted our relationship to be fun, exciting, and passionate. When you love someone, you do everything you can to keep the love alive, that's what I was doing with God. I wanted to keep our relationship alive. I didn't want to treat my relationship with God like I had other relationships. I knew that if I fell down that slippery slope our relationship would be over. The same way we make sacrifices to show our love to our children and spouse, the same way we should make sacrifices to show God that we are interested in doing life with him. God is looking to see if you're interested, because he is. The Bible says in 1 Samuel 16:7, "The

Lord does not look at the things people look at. People look at the outward appearance, but the Lord looks at the heart." We can demonstrate from the outside that we love God but if our heart doesn't match it, It will not impress God. As I spent more time with God, I began to let my heart do the speaking. God did not hold back, my heart was in full display, if he saw an area of my heart that needed work, he would let me know. It was up to me to make the changes. And because I loved God, I always worked towards the change. I wanted to honor God fully, every second I spent with him helped me better serve him. God was on my mind 24/7. That is what happens when we begin to fall in love with someone; we don't go a day without thinking about that person. For example, I think about my kids all the time. Everything that I do, I do it for my kids. The same sentiment began to occur when I said "Yes" to God, I started living for him.

Even when things did not make sense, I was living on purpose and for a purpose. I began to integrate things that drew me closer to God and I began to reject things that had nothing to do with my walk with Jesus. Jesus became my number one priority and I was ready to prove it to him. I exchanged listening to worldly music and began to listen to Gospel music. I also began watching sermons on a daily basis rather than TV shows. I lost interest in calling people on the phone. Instead I would rather read a book. Thankfully, God left some friends in my life. The friends I had left were all about God! Whenever we spoke on the phone it was usually about the latest thing God was doing in their lives. It was so easy to talk to them because we were on the same journey. It was so helpful to have friends who understood my walk and journey, God had been so good to me. God will do that, he will take some people out of your life and bring in new ones. New friends and opportunities that align with your calling. God knows the difficulty in walking with people who don't understand or put you down. God loves you and is always seeking a way to make you better!

When I look back at my life, all the things that happened to me good or bad was part of the plan.

When you are able to see things in a positive way, there's no way you will hold a grudge on anyone or dwell on the past. My life was and still is in God's hands and I trust him with whatever may come. When you put your trust in God instead of man, you will never be disappointed. Even my new friendships were a blessing! My new friends drew me closer to God they understood me, they prayed with me and strengthened my faith in God. I didn't understand God's plan then, but I do now. Now that I've come to terms with God's plan I am fully and solely concerned with advancing the Kingdom of God. I am careful with what I do, how I talk, what I think, and how I conduct my life. For instance, even my social media received a deep cleaning! I wanted to reflect who God was and use that platform to build the kingdom as well. My goal is to extend love and compassion, even though I am still a work in progress I have a responsibility to do right by God. If I mess up, I know I can always repent, apologize and not repeat the mistake again. We are not perfect, but day by day we will get better.

When you know who God is, you will want to resemble him. When you realize the sacrifice Jesus made on the cross, you will also begin to ask God how you can also serve him. After I said yes to the call of God, I knew I never wanted to return to who I was. I barely enjoyed my past, I worried so much, but now everything was in God's hands and I was at peace. I know God will never let me down. Even when God does not answer my prayer the way I expect it, I still trust him. With God by my side, I can finally live a stress free life because I know who God is. God is for me not against me. With God by my side I don't need to be anxious, I don't need to be in control, I don't need to worry, I just need to rely and obey whatever he instructs. I used to have full control over my finances, or so I thought. My control led me to sleepless nights, missing quality time with family, and overworking my body to pay a couple of bills. After I gave up my control and gave God full access into my life, I don't kill myself or spend sleepless nights trying to figure things out. Before I make a decision, I lay all my cares unto God and ask for direction. When God gives me an instruction, I trust and do as he says. The best part about communicating with God is his sincerity, when he sees you need help or correction in an area, he will always make it known to you. I've also learned the value of not complaining about my problems. When we focus on our hardships and don't let them go, we begin to put our hardships before God. Our hardship, our problems become our god. The more we complain about our problems the more we tell God that our problems are bigger than him. When in fact, we know, God is always greater and stronger! Instead of worrying and crying about the issue, I give it to God, I talk to God and trust that he will help me. Only God can care for me and make my hardships benefit me.

In my walk with God I've also learned how much I used to run to my friends first with my problems rather than to God. I sought my friend's advice, rather than seeking God. Now, when a problem presents itself, I first talk to God to hear what he has to say. I've done things on my terms for so long that I have grown weary, now I don't waste any time. I am thankful for all the setbacks and all the learning experiences. I know I wouldn't be here without God guiding me. I can honestly say I love my new life and I wouldn't trade it for anything in this world. When I married my husband, I vowed to always love him and do everything I could to make our relationship flourish. I said yes to a lifetime commitment with my husband. When God spoke to me and showed me my purpose, I also said yes to Him. I became one with God just like I am one with my husband. Everything that I do involve my husband. I don't make decisions without asking my husband. I care for my husband and show it to him on a daily basis. I do have bad days with my husband but I don't let it get in the way of our relationship. When we are away from each other, we stay in touch through phone calls, we are intentional about staying in communication. I trust him and know that he will not intentionally hurt me. The same way I care for my marriage, in the same way I care for my relationship with God. Saying yes to God has been the best decision I've ever made. I have no regrets in establishing a relationship with him. He is the love of my life, my creator, and stands above anyone and everything.

In everything that I do I involve God. I don't make any decisions without asking God and allowing him to give me feedback. Afterall, God is the best at giving advice! I do my very best to care for my husband through preparing healthy and delicious meals, now that is not something I can do for God but I do give him all my worship. You may be wondering, How do we worship God? I worship God through singing, dancing, keeping my prayer time, but most importantly through how I carry myself. In everything I do, I try my very best to represent God's love and grace. Unfortunately, I'm not perfect and I fail God many times a day but I always go to the feet of the father and repent and continue being my best for him. The best part of being one with God is that before I even say a word to him, he knows my heart. God is so close to me and cares about my every need. He will never hurt me or desert me. Unlike with my husband, my husband can leave and hurt me, God on the other hand won't ever! Even when I did not know God, he gave his only begotten Son for my sins. In my sin God loved me and still loves me. Saying yes to God has been the best decision I ever made. Saying "Yes" to God means you're done doing things your way and you're ready for a change. You're ready for God to show you who you are and what you've been called to do on this earth. Saying "Yes" doesn't necessarily mean you'll be involved in ministry per se. God may be calling you to continue being a Doctor, he may push you into enjoying your gifts as a teacher. At the end of the day, we need to be where the creator designed us to be.

Walking Into My Purpose

Walking within your calling will require you to step out of your comfort zone. It will take a lot of faith to walk out what God has called you to do. But you can do it, if God has called you to it he will walk you through it. In my case, many times I knew what I had to do but putting the first step forward was not the easiest for me. It was easy for me to begin to doubt myself. Thankfully, my time with God helped me understand who he had created me to be. God is a God of magnitude, without limit, without comparison, so anything that he will ask you to do will always resemble him. To us, the task may seem too big, but for him it probably could still be bigger. His ways are always going to be beyond our thinking, our imagination, and our comfort zone. God's big plan scares us because we just can't comprehend his ways, and that's ok, we just have to trust in God. God is seeking your small participation in the big plan because like always, he will handle the big stuff we can't. Walking in your purpose may seem scary but in reality, God will guide you through every step of the way. He will send the right people, the right connections at the right time. God will take care of you and everything pertaining to you, never doubt that. Don't be scared, talk to him, he wants to hear from you. A lot of times things don't happen right away but continue pressing and seeking God's voice, along the road, you will see the light. Along the road you may make the mistake of taking matters into your own hands because you may feel God is taking too long. Abraham and Sarah made a similar mistake they ran ahead of God and conceived a child without God's approval. If they would have just waited patiently, they would have avoided so much heartache. Remember, do not get distracted. God is always in control. The opportunity will not pass you by. Rely on God's timing. You will win the race. Your purpose will come to completion as long as you are patient and surrendered to God. Your experiences will stretch your faith and will prepare you for your purpose.

No one wants to die and not fulfill their purpose. Many times, we become angry and bitter at everyone around us because we know we're not living according to God's will. We marry the wrong person, we move to the wrong place, we take on the wrong job, the examples are endless. Some of us never even come to the realization that we are living outside of God's will because we are so prideful. When that happens, we die empty and we miss all the beautiful things that God had prepared for us. Doing what God has called you to do will leave you happy and fulfilled. Not doing God's will- will leave you drained and tired. Operating in your calling will give you a feeling of satisfaction. For example, If you are a teacher and doing a great job at teaching kids, you never give up on your kids and you love your job but you feel drained and deep down you feel like there is something else out there for you, then you are likely to be operating outside the calling for your life. Like myself, I had all the qualifications to be a nurse, I loved to help out others, I loved to make people feel better, I took great pleasure in cleaning a patient before bed, however, God had given me these traits to be somewhere else. God wanted me to help out a different population of sick people. God wanted me to help people who were sick spiritually instead of physically.

Regardless of who you are, God has already equipped you with everything you need including your passion. Consult with God, ask him to show you your calling. Follow your passions, because your passion may be hiding within your gifts. Not only will walking in your purpose makes you feel more alive, but when your time comes, you will be able to go in peace knowing you fulfilled your calling. The story in the Bible that we can refer to when we talk about our purpose is when Jesus met Simon Peter, James, and John, the sons of Zebedee. Luke 5:1-11, "They were out all night fishing and did not catch any fish, Jesus was preaching among the crowd and asked Peter Simon to put the boat out in the deep sea. Peter knowing that he had done that all night already and was unsuccessful, told Jesus I will do it because you said so. When they have done it, they caught so many fish that their net had broke. Simon Peter called his partners to come and help out and both boats started to sink because they had an abundant amount of fish." Man! This story never gets old for me. How are you a fisherman by profession, an expert at what you do, but unsuccessful in catching fish. Then comes Jesus, he tells you exactly where to go to catch fish and you catch an abundant amount! How did Jesus know exactly where to go to get the fish? Which tells me that whatever we are struggling with God already knows how to fix it. That little paycheck that you are running after every day, God knows how to give you money beyond what you need. The Bible says the boat began to sink because of all the fish. Which lets me understand that they caught an amount that they had never caught before! Peter fell to Jesus' feet and repented after he saw so many fish. For example, we are killing ourselves over $1,000 a week when God can give us that amount by the hour. You see, all we need is a word from God, because that one word can solve that one problem forever! Things that your previous generations were dealing with for decades, God can solve it for you just like he did for these fishermen. Can you imagine the amount of money they made in one day by listening to Jesus? Let's multiply that by 365 days! A lot of times we struggle because we don't seek advice from God. God can tell you exactly how to position yourself to receive breakthrough. What you can accomplish by leaning on your degree, your PHD, your doctorate, or even your lifetime occupation God can make you accomplish 10,000 times more than what you can do on your own when you listen to him. Therefore, seek him!

The fishermen were in shock after they realized how much fish they had caught. Jesus told them: "Don't be afraid, from now on you will be fisher of men." They pulled their boat up on shore, left everything and followed Jesus (Luke 5:1-11). God had a special calling on their life. Yes, they were fishermen but God had another plan for their life. They were fishermen by profession but God had told them their purpose. Secondly, God was using their passion to bring forth their purpose. Like I said before, God has already equipped you for everything he has called you to do. The fishermen knew how to get fish and were not afraid of the danger of the sea and the trade. Now that God had showed them their purpose, they were ready to implement their skills. Isn't it amazing how they were already working in the line of their calling? Another thing that stood out to me was the fact that these people were struggling until Jesus directed them to where they needed to go for an overflow of provision!

Imagine what your life would look like if you listened and obeyed God's voice, your life would take a turn for the better! The best part of this story was when Jesus asked them to "Follow" him. Basically, Jesus was saying, I can show you the best way to do what you do, but I can also show you what I have called you for! Your purpose! Will you follow Jesus into your purpose? The only way to hear his calling is by spending time with Him. This passage shows God's power and love for us. Jesus took the time to instruct his soon to be disciples. Sometimes what we may see as a roadblock is the perfect opportunity for God to do what only he can do. I was able to obey God because I took the time to listen to his voice, I leaned in and accepted what he had to say. I decided to follow the voice of God.

If everything in my past had been going great, I wouldn't have had a reason to listen to what God had to say. My focus would have been on what I could do for myself. Instead, God knew I was empty and helpless. God interfered, he wanted to bless me beyond my imagination. Even while you are uninterested about him, he still desires to work in you and for you. God can bless you and use you to bless others if you just let him. If you are worried about what following God may look like, look at my experience, I was concerned about my bills but God allowed me to pay every single one of them. God will not leave you, stay close to him. Where he leads, he will provide (Isaiah 58:11). Don't worry about leaving your comfort zone, let go of your control and let God lead you into your calling. What God has called you to do no one else can fulfill it but you. Don't let fear or worry stop you. God will share the steps to your calling with time, seek God for the details. As you walk with God, he will begin to reveal the steps necessary to achieve your purpose. You may be asking yourself why God doesn't just reveal it all to you in one sitting. Well, he doesn't give you everything at once because he wants you to keep coming back for guidance, remember you are a work in progress. If you don't have a relationship with God or distance yourself from spending time with him, chances are his will in your life will not come to fruition. God is so desperate and crazy in love with you that all he desires is to speak to you. God's love is real and genuine. God loves you. He knows your heart, you cannot fake your love for God. You can begin a relationship with God without wholeheartedly wanting one, but with time his presence is all you will ever desire. If you are struggling with desiring a relationship with Him but something inside of you would like to experience his company, ask God to show you how to love him and how to have a relationship with him and he will show you. The Holy Spirit will soften your heart and show you how to love God and how to open up to him. We cannot have a one-way relationship with God, we need his assistance. Once you start having a real relationship with God, it will be hard to stay away from him. If you ever begin to distance yourself from him, you will feel like you are missing something. God completes us, take a step closer to Him you won't ever regret it.

If God is so great, why don't more people answer the call of God in their life? Distractions, lack of wisdom, and unwillingness! Everyone has a purpose, but how do you know your purpose if you don't seek the answer to it? I didn't know I had a calling. I didn't know God wanted to use me to inspire, help, and teach others. I knew there was more to life, but I could never tell what it was. So, I kept living my life on my terms until the emptiness took over my being. I knew only God could help me figure my life out. No one taught me how to seek God or how to speak to God. I was not exposed to the word of God, my family didn't know any better. My family taught me how to seek a job, an education, and a career but not my purpose. Now that I know better, I will definitely teach my kids and my kids will teach their kids. Our future generations will know they have a purpose, most importantly that God loves them and desires to speak to them.

Another reason behind the hesitation of answering the call of God is the thought that God is boring or too demanding. Some individuals simply do not want to give up their control. They are not willing to sacrifice or compromise their current lifestyle. They are far away from God and have no intention to get closer to him. While they don't worship the real God their creator they worship other Gods. They worship money, women, men, alcohol, their job, fashion, their family, and so on. You may not physically worship your money but if it puts God second then that thing is your God.

Following your purpose requires you step out on faith. It requires you to step out of your comfort zone. Unfortunately, many times people don't follow their purpose because they can't let go of control. If you think you don't know the right people or have the right amount of money to do what God has called you to do, let me tell you this, God will make a way! Kick worry to the side, work in obedience to his word. If God asks you to start a project and you don't take the initiative to get started, you are in disobedience. Remember God's ways are greater than yours, simply obey. Can you imagine if Noah had not obeyed God! Even though everything seemed ridiculous, Noah obeyed. When it finally began to rain, Noah knew his obedience was not in vain. Sometimes you won't understand and those around you will look at you weird, but if God asks you to do something, then do it. Say yes to the adventure with God, he has your back.

Words of Wisdom

"What do you want to be when you grow up?" That is the most common question asked to children as soon as they learn how to speak. Society teaches us to look for a profession, something that will make us a productive member of society. Being a productive member of society is great, however, what about your purpose? No one ever asked me that question growing up. What is your purpose? Instead, as an adult I heard at least one thousand times, what is your profession? Having a profession is important, it helps and guarantees a better job, opens doors for great opportunities, and also helps you take care of your finances. A purpose on the other hand is what makes you unique! Your purpose is what you were created to do and be, it is your mission on this earth. While having a profession is great, having a purpose is even greater. Many of us spend money studying a profession and end up doing something else. In other cases, people spend money paying for college tuition and end up in a job they are not happy with. Everyone is looking for happiness comes from doing what you were created to do on earth. In your mother's womb, God has placed a purpose inside of you. Just like Jesus had a mission on this earth, so do we. Money will never complete you, your purpose will! Purpose is that thing that we all have inside of us that we love to do so much that we dream about it all the time and we would be willing to do it even if we never saw a paycheck. The only way to find and receive confirmation of what your purpose is, is through spending time with God. He will walk you through the plan for your life. God is the only one who has a plan for your life. Don't try to figure things out on your own, you will be wasting time and only grow weary. Trust God and seek his voice. Life is too precious to let it go without living it to the fullest. Take advantage of your time, any chance you get, spend it with God. God is more important than anything the world can offer. Seek God with all your heart. He will reveal secrets, challenges, and solutions along the way. He can even show you who your spouse is! Make God a priority and continue to walk with him daily, he will guide your every step Even when it may seem like you are not moving ahead, don't worry because the one who created the whole world and everything inside of it is preceding your steps.